I0801603

SUBLIMITAS ET MISERIA HOMINIS

ON THE GRANDEUR AND MISERY OF MAN

SUBLIMITAS ET MISERIA HOMINIS

ON THE GRANDEUR AND MISERY OF MAN

APOSTOLIC LETTER

On the Fourth Centenary
of the Birth of Blaise Pascal

POPE FRANCIS

Our Sunday Visitor
Huntington, Indiana

Published 2023 by Our Sunday Visitor Publishing

28 27 26 25 24 23 1 2 3 4 5 6 7 8 9

Our Sunday Visitor Publishing Division, Our Sunday Visitor, Inc., 200 Noll Plaza, Huntington, IN 46750; 1-800-348-2440; www.osv.com.

ISBN: 978-1-63966-190-9 (Inventory T2886)
eISBN: 978-1-63966-191-6

Cover design: Tyler Ottinger
Cover art: Adobe Stock
Interior design: Amanda Falk

PRINTED IN THE UNITED STATES OF AMERICA

THE GRANDEUR AND MISERY OF MAN. This paradox is central to the thought and enduring message of Blaise Pascal, born four centuries ago, on June 19, 1623, in Clermont in central France. From childhood, Pascal devoted his life to the pursuit of truth. By the use of reason, he sought its traces in the fields of mathematics, geometry, physics, and philosophy, making remarkable discoveries and attaining great fame even at an early age. Yet he was not content with those achievements. In a century of great advances in many fields of science, accompanied by a growing spirit of philosophical and religious scepticism, Blaise Pascal proved to be a tireless seeker of truth, a "restless" spirit, open to ever new and greater horizons.

Pascal's brilliant and inquisitive mind never ceased to ponder the question, ancient yet ever new, that wells up in the human heart: "What is man that you are mindful of him, the son of man that you care for him?" (Ps 8:5). This question has perplexed men and women of every time and place, every culture, language and religion. "What is man in nature?" Pascal asks. "Nothing with respect to the infinite, yet everything with respect to nothing."[1] The question had been posed by the psalmist in the context of the history of love between God and his people, a history culminating in the incarnation of the "son of man," Jesus Christ, whom the Father gave up to forsakenness in order to crown him with glory and honor above every creature (cf. v. 6). To this question, raised in a language so different from that of mathematics and geometry, Pascal continued to devote his attention.

For this reason, I believe that it is fitting to describe Pascal as a man marked by a fundamental attitude of awe and openness to all reality. Openness to other dimensions of knowledge and life, openness to others, openness to society. For example, in 1661 he developed, in Paris, the first public transport system in history, the "five-penny coaches." If I mention this at the beginning of this letter, it is to make clear that neither his conversion to Christ, which began with the "night of fire" on November 23, 1654, nor his masterful intellectual defense of the Christian faith, made him any less a man of his time. He continued to be concerned with the questions that troubled his age and with the material needs of all the members of the society in which he lived.

This openness to the world around him kept him concerned for others even in his final illness, at only thirty-nine years of age. At this, the last stage of his earthly pilgrimage, he is reported to have said, "If the physicians tell the truth, and God grants that I recover from this sickness, I am resolved to have no other work or occupation for the rest of my life except to serve the poor."[2] It is moving to realize that in the last days of his life, so great a genius as Blaise Pascal saw nothing more pressing than the need to devote his energies to works of mercy: *"The sole object of Scripture is charity."*[3]

I am pleased that on this, the fourth centenary of his birth, God's providence grants me this opportunity to pay homage to Pascal, and to recall those aspects of his life and thought that I deem helpful to encourage Christians in our day, and their contemporaries of good will, in the pursuit of authentic happiness. For "all people seek to be happy. This is true without exception, whatever the different means they employ. All tend to the same goal."[4] Four centuries after his birth, Pascal remains our traveling companion, accompanying our quest for true happiness and, through the gift of faith, our humble and joyful recognition of the crucified and risen Lord.

A man in love with Christ, who speaks to everyone

If Blaise Pascal can attract everyone, it is above all because he spoke so convincingly of our human condition. Yet it would be mistaken to see in him merely an insightful observer of human behavior. His monumental *Pensées*, [which includes some] individual aphorisms [that] remain famous, cannot really be understood unless we realize that Jesus Christ and sacred Scripture are both their center and the key to their understanding. For if Pascal proposed to speak of man and God, it was because he had arrived at the certainty that "not only do we know God solely through Jesus Christ, but we know ourselves solely through Jesus Christ. We do not know life and death except through

Jesus Christ. Apart from Jesus Christ, we understand neither our life nor our death, neither God nor ourselves. Hence without the Scriptures, which speak solely of Jesus Christ, we know nothing, and we see only darkness."[5] If this daring statement is to be understood by all, and not considered a purely dogmatic assertion incomprehensible to those who do not share the Church's faith, or a disparagement of the legitimate scope of natural reason, it needs to be clarified.

Faith, love, and freedom

As Christians, we need to avoid the temptation to present our faith as an incontestable certainty evident to everyone. Clearly, Pascal was concerned to make people realize that "God and truth are inseparable,"[6] yet he also knew that belief is possible only by the grace of God, embraced by a heart that is free. Through faith he had personally encountered "the God of Abraham, the God of Isaac, the God of Jacob, not the God of the philosophers and the learned,"[7] and had acknowledged Jesus Christ as "the way, and the truth, and the life" (Jn 14:6). For this reason, I would suggest that everyone who wishes to persevere in seeking truth — a never-ending task in this life — should listen to Blaise Pascal, a man of prodigious intelligence who insisted that apart from the aspiration to love, no truth is worthwhile. "We make truth itself into an idol, for truth apart from charity is not God, but his image; it is an idol which must in no way be loved or worshiped."[8]

Pascal would thus shield us from the false teachings, superstitions, and libertinism that avert so many people from the lasting peace and joy of the One who desires that we should choose "life and good," not "death and evil" (Dt 30:15, 19). Yet the tragedy of this life is that we at times fail to see clearly, and as a result we choose poorly. For we cannot savor the joy of the Gospel unless "the Holy Spirit fills us with his power and frees us from our weakness, our selfishness, our complacency, and our pride."[9] What is more, "without the wisdom of discernment, we can become prey to every passing trend."[10] That is why an appreciation of the living faith of Blaise Pascal, who sought to demonstrate that the Christian religion is "venerable because it truly knows man," and "lovable because it promises true good,"[11] can help us make our way through the shadows and sorrows of this world.

An outstanding scientific mind

When his mother died in 1626, Blaise Pascal was three years old. His father, Étienne, a well-known jurist, was also renowned for his notable scientific gifts, particularly in the fields of mathematics and geometry. Choosing to provide personally for the education of his three children, Jacqueline, Blaise, and Gilberte, he moved to Paris in 1632. Very quickly, Blaise showed exceptional intelligence and persistence in seeking truth. His sister Gilberte tells us that, "from childhood, he could only accept things that struck him as evidently true; as a result, when not provided with good reasons, he sought them himself."[12] One day his father found Blaise studying geometry and suddenly realized that, without knowing that the same theorems could be found in books under other names, Blaise, at age twelve, entirely on his own, by drawing figures on the ground, had demonstrated the first thirty-two propositions of Euclid.[13] Gilberte recalled that their father was "astounded at the depth and the power of his intellect."[14]

In the years that followed, Blaise Pascal worked intensely to make his immense talent bear fruit. At seventeen, he was in communication with the most learned men of his time. In quick succession came his discoveries and his publications. In 1642, at the age of nineteen, he invented an arithmetic machine, the ancestor of our modern computers. In this regard, Pascal speaks to our own times, for he reminds us of the grandeur of human reason and encourages us to employ it in understanding the mysteries of the world around us. His grasp of mathematics, the ability to understand in detail how things work, would prove helpful to him throughout his life. In the words of the eminent theologian Hans Urs von Balthasar: "He trained himself in the precision appropriate to mathematics and natural science as such, so as to attain that quite other precision appropriate to the realm of being and to the Christian realm."[15] Pascal's confidence in the use of natural reason, which unites him to all seekers of truth, enabled him both to acknowledge its limits and to be receptive to the supernatural reasons of divine revelation with that sense of paradox that was to find expression in the philosophical depth and literary charm of his *Pensées*. "The Church expended as much effort in demonstrating that Jesus Christ was man against those who denied this as she did in demonstrating that he was God; and both were equally evident."[16]

The philosophers

Many of Pascal's writings are steeped in the language of philosophy. This is especially true of his *Pensées*, the collection of fragments, published posthumously, that are his notes and sketches for a philosophy inspired by a theological concern. Scholars have attempted, with varying results, to restore the collection's original form and unity. Pascal's passionate love for Christ and for serving the poor, which I mentioned earlier, were not so much the sign of a disconnect in the mind of this bold disciple, as of a deeper growth toward evangelical radicalism, a progression, aided by grace, toward the living truth of the Lord. Pascal, who possessed the supernatural certitude of faith and considered it fully compatible with reason while infinitely surpassing the latter, sought as much as possible to engage in dialogue with those who did not share his faith. For "to those who do not have faith, we cannot give it except by reasoning, as we wait for God to give it to them by moving their heart."[17] Here we see a completely respectful and patient form of evangelization that our generation would do well to imitate.

It is necessary then, for a proper understanding of Pascal's thinking on Christianity, to be attentive to his philosophy. He admired the wisdom of the ancient Greek philosophers, who sought with simplicity and tranquillity to live well as citizens of a polis: "We think of Plato and Aristotle as wearing the flowing robes of scholars. They were normal people, like everyone else, who enjoyed a good laugh with their friends. When they were composing their *Laws* and *Politics*, they did it for pleasure. It was the least philosophical and least serious part of their life; the most philosophical part was to live simply and peaceably."[18] Yet for all their greatness and their usefulness, Pascal recognized the limits of those philosophies: Stoicism leads to pride;[19] scepticism to despair.[20] Human reason is a marvel of creation, which sets man apart from all other creatures, for "man is but a reed, the weakest in nature, yet he is a thinking reed."[21] The limits of the philosophers are thus, quite simply, the limits of created reason. Democritus might well say, "I am going to speak about everything,"[22] but reason cannot, of itself, resolve the deepest and most urgent issues. In the end, both for the age of Pascal as well as for our own, what remains the greatest and most pressing question? It is that of the overall meaning of our destiny, our life, and our hope, which is directed to a happiness that we are not forbidden to imagine as eternal, but which God alone can grant: "Nothing is as important to man as his own state; nothing to him is as fearsome as eternity."[23]

In reflecting on Pascal's *Pensées*, we constantly encounter, in one way or another, this fundamental principle: "reality is superior to ideas." Pascal teaches us to keep our distance from "various means of masking reality," from "angelic forms of purity" to "intellectual discourse bereft of wisdom."[24] Nothing is more dangerous than a disembodied reason: "He who would act as an angel, acts as a beast."[25] The baneful ideologies from which we continue to suffer in the areas of economics, social life, anthropology, and morality keep their followers imprisoned in a world of illusions, where ideas have replaced reality.

The human condition

Pascal's philosophy, ever paradoxical, is grounded in an approach as simple as it is lucid: It seeks to attain to "reality illumined by reason."[26] He starts by observing that man is in some way a stranger to himself, at once great and wretched. Great by virtue of his reason and his ability to master his passions, but great too "in that he acknowledges himself wretched."[27] Indeed, man aspires to something other than satisfying or resisting his instincts, "for what is nature to animals, we call wretchedness in man."[28] An intolerable disproportion exists between, on the one hand, our limitless desire for happiness and knowledge of truth, and, on the other, our limited reason and physical frailty, which ultimately ends in death. Pascal's strength is also his relentless realism: "It does not take great intelligence to realize that here below there is no true and solid satisfaction, that all our pleasures are but vanity, that our ills are infinite, and that death, which threatens us constantly, will infallibly set before us, in a few years, the dread alternative of being annihilated or of being unhappy for all eternity. Nothing is more real than that, nor more frightening. We can act as bravely as we like: This is the end that awaits the finest life in the world."[29] In this tragic condition, surely an individual cannot retreat into himself, for his wretchedness and the uncertainty of his destiny prove unbearable to him. As a result, he needs to distract himself. Pascal readily acknowledges this: "Hence it is that men so greatly love noise and commotion."[30] For if a person does not divert himself from his condition — and we know very well how to divert ourselves by work, forms of leisure, relationships in family or among friends, but also, alas, by the vices to which certain passions lead — his humanity experiences "its nothingness, its abandonment, its insufficiency, its dependence, its powerlessness, its emptiness. [And there emerge] from the depths of his soul ennui, melancholy, sadness, chagrin, spite, despair."[31] Diversion fails to satisfy, much less fulfill, our great desire for life and happiness. This is something that all of us know quite well.

At this point, Pascal sets forth his great argument: "What is it, then, that this longing and this feeling of helplessness cry out to us, if not that man once enjoyed a true happiness, of which there now remains but an empty trace that he tries in vain to fill with everything around him, seeking in things he lacks what he cannot obtain from those he has. Yet none of these can provide it, for this infinite abyss cannot be bridged except by an infinite and immutable object, which is God himself."[32] If man is like "a dispossessed king,"[33] seeking only to recover his lost grandeur while knowing that he is incapable of doing so, then what is he? "What a fantastic creature is man, a novelty, a monstrosity, chaotic, contradictory, prodigious, judge of all things, feeble earthworm, bearer of truth, mire of uncertainty and error, glory and refuse of the universe! Who can undo this tangle?"[34] As a philosopher,

Pascal saw clearly that "the greater our intelligence, the more we discover man's grandeur and his baseness,"[35] and that these contradictions are irreconcilable. Human reason cannot make them agree, nor resolve the enigma.

Pascal goes on to argue that if there is a God, and if man has received a divine revelation — as a number of religions profess — and if that revelation is true, it must contain the answer we await in order to resolve the contradictions that cause us such anguish. "The greatness and wretchedness of man are so evident that the true religion must necessarily teach us both that there is in man a great principle of grandeur and a great principle of wretchedness. It must also account for these astonishing contradictions."[36] From his study of the great religions, Pascal concludes that "no thought and no ascetic-mystical practice can offer a way of redemption," unless by "the higher criterion of truth found in the illumination of grace."[37] "It is in vain," Pascal writes, imagining what the true God might tell us, "that you seek in yourselves the remedy for your miseries. All your intelligence could only attain the knowledge that it is not in yourselves that you will find either truth or goodness. The philosophers promised it to you, and they were unable to deliver. They know neither what is your true good, nor your veritable state."[38]

After applying his extraordinary intelligence to the study of the human condition, the sacred Scriptures, and the Church's tradition, Pascal now presents himself with childlike simplicity as a humble witness of the Gospel. As a Christian, he wishes to speak of Jesus Christ to those who have hastily concluded that there is no solid reason to believe in the truths of Christianity. For his part, he knows from experience that the content of divine revelation is not only *not* opposed to the demands of reason, but offers the amazing response that no philosophy could ever attain on its own.

Conversion: The visit of the Lord

On November 23, 1654, Pascal had a powerful experience that even now is referred to as his "night of fire." This mystical experience, which caused him to weep tears of joy, was so intense and so decisive for him that he recorded it on a piece of paper, precisely dated, the "Memorial," which he inserted in the lining of his coat, only to be discovered after his death. While it is impossible to know the exact nature of what took place in Pascal's soul that night, it seems to have been an encounter which he himself acknowledged as analogous to the encounter, fundamental for the whole history of revelation and salvation, that Moses experienced in the presence of the burning bush (cf. Ex 3). The term "FIRE,"[39] which Pascal placed as the heading of the "Memorial," invites us, relatively speaking, to make this comparison. The parallel would seem to be indicated by Pascal himself who, immediately after the evocation of fire, repeated the appellation that the Lord gave himself in the presence of Moses — "the God of Abraham, the God of Isaac, the God of Jacob" (Ex 3:6, 15) — and then added: "not of the philosophers and the sages. Certainty. Certainty. Feeling. Joy. Peace. God of Jesus Christ."

Our God is indeed joy, and Blaise Pascal testifies to this before the whole Church and before all those who seek God. "This is not the abstract God or the cosmic God, no. This is the God of a person, of a call, the God of Abraham, Isaac, and Jacob, the God who is certitude, who is sentiment, who is joy."[40] The encounter that night, which confirmed for Pascal the "grandeur of the human soul," overwhelmed him with that same lively and fathomless joy: "Joy, joy, joy, tears of joy." And that divine joy became for him an occasion of confession and prayer: "Jesus Christ. I separated myself from him. I fled him, denied him, crucified him. May I never be separated from him."[41] Pascal's experience of the love of God, who in Jesus Christ personally shared in our history and ceaselessly shares in our life, set Pascal on the path of profound conversion, a life of charity and thus the "complete and sweet renunciation"[42] of the "old self, corrupt and deluded by its lusts" (Eph 4:22).

As St. John Paul II noted in his encyclical on the relationship of faith and reason, "philosophers such as Pascal" are outstanding for their rejection of all presumption, as well as for their stance of humility and courage. They came to realize that "faith liberates reason from presumption."[43] Certainly, prior to the night of November 23, 1654, Pascal "never doubted the existence of God. He also knew that God is the supreme good. … What he lacked and longed for was not knowledge but power; not truth, but strength."[44] That strength was now bestowed on him by grace, and he felt himself drawn with certitude and joy to Jesus Christ: "We know God only through Jesus Christ. Without this mediator, all communication with God is taken away."[45] To discover Jesus Christ is to discover the Savior and Liberator whom I need: "This God is nothing other than the redeemer of our miseries. Thus we can only really know God by knowing our iniquities."[46] As with every authentic conversion, the conversion of Blaise Pascal took place in humility, which delivers us "from our narrowness and self-absorption."[47]

The vast and restless intelligence of Blaise Pascal, brimming with peace and joy at the revelation of Jesus Christ, invites us, following "the order of the heart,"[48] to advance toward the brightness of "these heavenly lights."[49] For if our God is a "hidden God" (cf. Is 45:15), it is because he "willed to conceal himself"[50] in such a way that our reason, illumined by grace, will never stop seeking to find him. Hence, it is by the illumination of grace that we come to know him. Yet our human freedom must be open to this, and indeed Jesus comforts us with these words: "You would not seek me if you had not found me."[51]

The order of the heart and its reasons for believing

In the words of Pope Benedict XVI, "the Catholic tradition from the beginning has rejected what is called fideism, which is the desire to believe against reason."[52] Pascal is likewise deeply attached to the "reasonableness of faith in God,"[53] not only because "the mind cannot be forced to believe what it knows to be false,"[54] but also because, "if we contradict the principles of reason, our religion would be absurd and ridiculous."[55] Yet while faith is reasonable, it remains a gift of God and may not be imposed. "We do not prove that we should be loved by setting out the reasons why; that would be ridiculous,"[56] Pascal tells us with his subtle humor, comparing human love and the way that

God beckons us. Like human love, which proposes but never imposes — the love of God never imposes itself.[57] Jesus bore witness to the truth (cf. Jn 18:37), but "refused to use force to impose it on those who spoke out against it."[58] That is why "there is enough light for those who desire only to see, and enough darkness for those disposed otherwise."[59]

Pascal goes on to say that "faith differs from proof. One is human, while the other is God's gift."[60] Hence, it is impossible to believe "unless God inclines the heart."[61] Although faith is of a higher order than reason, it does not follow that faith is opposed to reason; rather, faith infinitely surpasses reason. In reading Pascal's work, we do not first encounter reason that clarifies faith, but a Christian of great logical rigor accounting for an order, graciously established by God, which transcends reason: "The infinite distance between bodies and minds represents the infinitely more infinite distance between minds and charity, for the latter is supernatural."[62] As a scientist expert in geometry — the science of bodies positioned in space — and a mathematician expert in philosophy — the science of minds positioned in history — Blaise Pascal, enlightened by the grace of faith, could sum up his whole experience in these words: "From all bodies put together, one could not succeed in producing a tiny thought. That is impossible and of another order. From all bodies and minds, one could not draw an impulse of true charity. That is impossible and of another supernatural order."[63]

Neither the operations of geometry nor philosophical reasoning permit us, of themselves, to arrive at a "very clear view" of the world or of ourselves. Those enmeshed in the details of their calculations do not benefit from the view of the whole that enables us to "see all the principles." That is the task of the "spirit of finesse" which Pascal extols, for in attempting to grasp reality, "one must immediately take things in at a single glance."[64] This intuitive vision has to do with what Pascal calls the "heart": "We know the truth not only by reason but even more by the heart; it is by the latter that we come to know the first principles, and it is in vain that reasoning, which has no part in it, tries to refute them."[65] Divinely revealed truths — such as the fact that the God who created us is love, that he is Father, Son and Holy Spirit, and that he became incarnate in Jesus Christ, who died and rose for our salvation — are not demonstrable by reason. They can only be known by the certitude of faith, and then pass immediately from the spiritual heart to the rational mind, which acknowledges their truth and can explicate them in turn. "This is why those to whom God has given religious faith by moving their hearts are blessed indeed and rightly convinced."[66]

Pascal never grew resigned to the fact that some men and women not only do not know Jesus Christ, but disdain, out of laziness or due to their passions, to take the Gospel seriously. For in Jesus Christ their very lives are at stake. "The immortality of the soul is so important to us, something that touches us so deeply, that we need to have lost all feeling to be unconcerned with knowing what is at stake. … And that is why, among those who are not convinced about this, I would distinguish clearly between those who make every effort to investigate it and those who go about their lives without being concerned about it or thinking of it."[67] We know very well that often we attempt to flee death, or to overcome it, thinking that we can "banish the thought of our finite existence" or "remove its power and dispel fear. But Christian faith is not a way of exorcizing the fear of death; rather, it helps us to face death. Sooner or later, we will all pass through that door. … The true light that illumines the mystery of death comes from the resurrection of Christ."[68] Only God's grace enables the human heart to know God and to live a life of charity. This led an important commentator on Pascal in our own day to write that "thought does not become Christian unless it attains to that which Jesus Christ brought about, which is charity."[69]

Pascal, controversy, and charity

Before concluding, I must mention Pascal's relationship to Jansenism. One of his sisters, Jacqueline, had entered religious life in Port-Royal, in a religious congregation the theology of which was greatly influenced by Cornelius Jansen, whose treatise *Augustinus* appeared in 1640. In January 1655, following his "night of fire," Pascal made a retreat at the abbey of Port-Royal. In the months that followed, an important and lengthy dispute about *Augustinus* arose between Jesuits and "Jansenists" at the Sorbonne, the university of Paris. The controversy dealt chiefly with the question of God's grace and the relationship between grace and human nature, specifically our free will. Pascal, while not a member of the congregation of Port-Royal, nor given to taking sides — as he wrote, "I am alone. ... I am not at all part of Port-Royal"[70] — was charged by the Jansenists to defend them, given his outstanding rhetorical skill. He did so in 1656 and 1657, publishing a series of eighteen writings known as *The Provincial Letters*.

Although several propositions considered "Jansenist" were indeed contrary to the faith,[71] a fact that Pascal himself acknowledged, he maintained that those propositions were not present in *Augustinus* or held by those associated with Port-Royal. Even so, some of his own statements, such as those on predestination, drawn from the later theology of Augustine and formulated more severely by Jansen, do not ring true. We should realize, however, that, just as Saint Augustine sought in the fifth century to combat the Pelagians, who claimed that man can, by his own powers and without God's grace, do good and be saved, so Pascal, for his part, sincerely believed that he was battling an implicit Pelagianism or semi-Pelagianism in the teachings of the "Molinist" Jesuits, named after the theologian Luis de Molina, who had died in 1600 but was still quite influential in the middle of the seventeenth century. Let us credit Pascal with the candor and sincerity of his intentions.

This letter is no place to reopen the question. Even so, what Pascal rightly warned against remains a source of concern for our own age: a "neo-Pelagianism"[72] that would make everything depend on "human effort channelled by ecclesial rules and structures"[73] and can be recognized by the fact that it "intoxicates us with the presumption of a salvation earned through our own efforts."[74] It should also be pointed out that Pascal's final position on grace, and in particular the fact that God "desires everyone to be saved and to come to the knowledge of the truth" (1 Tm 2:4), was set out in perfectly Catholic terms at the end of his life.[75]

As I noted earlier, Blaise Pascal, at the conclusion of a life that was brief yet extraordinarily rich and fruitful, set the love of his brothers and sisters above all else. He felt and knew that he was a member of one body, for "God, having made the heaven and the earth which are not conscious of the happiness of their existence, wished to create beings who would know that happiness and constitute a body of thinking members."[76] Pascal, as a lay Christian, savored the joy of the Gospel with which the Spirit wishes to heal and make fruitful "every aspect of humanity" and to bring "all men and women together at table in God's kingdom."[77] When, in 1659, he composed his magnificent *Prayer to Ask of God the Proper Use of Sickness*, Pascal was a man at peace, no longer engaged in controversies or even apologetics. Gravely ill and at the point of dying, he asked to receive holy Communion, but that was not immediately possible. So he asked his sister, "since I cannot communicate in the head [Jesus Christ], I would like to communicate in the members."[78] He "greatly desired to die in the company of the poor."[79] It was said of Pascal, shortly after he took his last breath on August 19, 1662, that "he died with the simplicity of a child."[80] After receiving the sacraments, his last words were, "May God never abandon me."[81]

May the brilliant work of Blaise Pascal and the example of his life, so profoundly immersed in Jesus Christ, help us to persevere to the end on the path of truth, conversion, and charity. For this life passes away in a moment: "Everlasting joy in return for a single day's effort on earth."[82]

Rome, Basilica of St. John Lateran, June 19, 2023

NOTES

1. Blaise Pascal, *Pensées*, B 72, L 199. In the citations of the *Pensées* that follow, the letters B and L refer, respectively, to the Brunschvicg and Lafuma numberings.

2. Gilberte Périer, "Vie de M. Pascal," in *Oeuvres complètes*, par M. Le Guern, I (Paris: 1998), 91.

3. *Pensées*, B 670, L 270.

4. Ibid., B 425, L 148.

5. Ibid., B 546, L 417.

6. Pascal, "Entretien avec M. de Sacy," in *Oeuvres complètes*, par Michel Le Guern, II (Paris: 2000), 90.

7. *Pensées* (Mémorial), L 913.

8. *Pensées* (Le Mystère de Jésus), B 582, L 926.

9. Francis, apostolic exhortation *Gaudete et Exsultate*, 65.

10. Ibid., 167.

11. *Pensées*, B 187, L 12.

12. Périer, op. cit., 64.

13. Cf. ibid., 65.

14. Ibid.

15 . Hans Urs von Balthasar, "Pascal" in *The Glory of the Lord, A Theological Aesthetics III: Lay Styles* (San Francisco: Ignatius Press; New York: Crossroads Publications, 1986) p. 182.

16. *Pensées*, B 764, L 307.

17. Ibid., B 282, L 110.

18. Ibid., B 331, L 533.

19. Pascal, "Entretien avec M. de Sacy," op. cit., 98.

20. Cf. *Pensées*, B 435, L 208.

21. Ibid., B 347, L 200.

22. Ibid., B 72, L 199.

23. Ibid., B 194, L 427.

24. Francis, apostolic exhortation *Evangelii Gaudium*, 231.

25. *Pensées*, B 358, L 678.

26. *Evangelii Gaudium*, 232.

27. *Pensées*, B 397, L 114.

28. Ibid., B 409, L 117.
29. Ibid., B 194, L 427.
30. Ibid., B 139, L 136.
31. Ibid., B 131, L 622.
32. Ibid., B 425, L 148.
33. Ibid., B 398, L 116.
34. Ibid., B 434, L 131.
35. Ibid., B 443, L 613.
36. Ibid., B 430, L 149.
37. Von Balthasar, op. cit., p. 186.
38. *Pensées*, B 430, L 149.
39. *Pensées* (Mémorial), L 913.
40. Francis, General Audience, June 3, 2020.
41. *Pensées* (Mémorial), L 913.
42. Ibid., L 913.
43. John Paul II, encyclical *Fides et Ratio* (September 14, 1998), 76.
44. Henri Gouhier, *Blaise Pascal: commentaires* (Paris: Vrin, 1971), 44-45.
45. *Pensées*, B 547, L 189.
46. Ibid.
47. *Evangelii Gaudium*, 8.
48. Cf. *Pensées*, B 283, L 298.
49. Ibid., B 435, L 208.
50. Ibid., B 585, L 242.
51. *Pensées* (Le Mystère de Jésus), B 553, L 919.
52. Benedict XVI, General Audience, November 21, 2012.
53. Ibid.
54. "Entretien avec M. de Sacy," op. cit., p. 87
55. *Pensées*, B 273, L 173.
56. Ibid., B 283, L 298.
57. Cf. Homily for the Solemnity of Our Lord Jesus Christ, King of the Universe, November 20, 2022.
58. Second Vatican Council, *Dignitatis Humanae*, 11.
59. *Pensées*, B 430, L 149.
60. Ibid., B 248, L 7.
61. Ibid., B 284, L 380.
62. Ibid., B 793, L 308.
63. Ibid., B 793, L 308.

64. Ibid., B 1, L 512.

65. Ibid., B 282, L 110.

66. Ibid.

67. Ibid., B 194, L 427.

68. Francis, General Audience, February 9, 2022.

69. Jean-Luc Marion, *La Métaphysique et après*, (Paris: Grasset, 2023), 356.

70. "Dix-septième lettre provinciale," in *Oeuvres complètes*, par Le Guern, II (Paris: 2000), 781.

71. Cf. Bruno Neveu, *L'erreur et son juge: remarques sur les censures doctrinales à l'époque moderne*, (Naples, Italy: Bibliopolis, 1993).

72. Cf. Congregation for the Doctrine of the Faith, letter *Placuit Deo*, February 22, 2018; *Gaudete et Exsultate*, 57–59.

73. *Gaudete et Exsultate*, 59.

74. Francis, apostolic letter *Desiderio Desideravi*, 20.

75. Cf. *Pensées* (Le Mystère de Jésus), B 550, L 931. The initial words — "I love all men as my brothers, because all are redeemed" — are crossed out in the Lafuma edition.

76. Ibid., B 482, L 360.

77. *Evangelii Gaudium*, 237.

78. Périer, op. cit., pp. 92-93.

79. Ibid., op. cit., p. 93.

80. Ibid., op. cit., p. 90.

81. Ibid., op. cit., p. 94.

82. *Pensées* (Mémorial), L 913.

You might also like:

DIVERSE YET UNITED:

Communicating Truth in Charity

By Pope Francis

With a Foreword by Kevin C. Rhoades, Bishop of Fort Wayne-South Bend, and a Preface by Justin Welby, Archbishop of Canterbury

As disciples of Jesus Christ, we are called to dialogue and encounter. We are expected to be welcoming and open to all people, including those who think differently from us or who hold conflicting opinions. We are also called to share the Truth, which is God's love for us in Jesus Christ.

"[Jesus] asks us not to fix our gaze on what divides us, but rather on what unites us, seeking to know and love Jesus better and to share the richness of his love," Pope Francis writes in *Diverse Yet United: Communicating Truth in Charity.*

Available at
OSVCatholicBookstore.com
or wherever books are sold